Every Kid's Guide to
Nutrition and Health Care

Written by
JOY BERRY

CHILDRENS PRESS ®
CHICAGO

About the Author and Publisher

Joy Berry's mission in life is to help families cope with everyday problems and to help children become competent, responsible, happy individuals. To achieve her goal, she has written over two hundred self-help books for children from birth through age twelve. Her work revolutionized children's publishing by providing families with practical, how-to, living skills information that was previously unavailable in children's books.

   Joy gathered a dedicated team of experts, including psychologists, educators, child developmentalists, writers, editors, designers, and artists, to form her publishing company and to help produce her work.

   The company, Living Skills Press, produces thoroughly researched books and audio-visual materials that successfully combine humor and education to teach subjects ranging from how to clean a bedroom to how to resolve problems and get along with other people.

Managing Editor: Ellen Klarberg
Copy Editor: Kate Dickey
Contributing Editors: Libby Byers, Nancy Cochran, Maureen Dryden,
Yona Flemming, Kathleen Mohr, Susan Motycka
Editorial Assistant: Sandy Passarino

Art Director: Laurie Westdahl
Design: Abigail Johnston, Laurie Westdahl
Production: Abigail Johnston
Illustrations designed by: Bartholomew
Inker: Berenice Happe Iriks
Colorer: Berenice Happe Iriks
Composition: Curt Chelin

Your body is a wonderful organism that needs certain things to keep it alive and well.

In **EVERY KID'S GUIDE TO NUTRITION AND HEALTH CARE,** you will learn how to care for your body and why your body needs

- good food,
- water,
- exercise,
- air and sunshine,
- proper clothing,
- adequate shelter,
- cleanliness, and
- rest and sleep.

Your body needs *good food*.

Good food helps make it possible for your body to stay alive and well.

Your body needs *protein.* Protein helps your body grow and become strong. Protein also helps your body stay well.

Here are some foods that provide protein: fish, poultry, meat, milk, cheese, eggs, and certain combinations of grains, beans, peas, and lentils.

Your body needs *carbohydrates.* Carbohydrates give your body energy.

Here are some foods that provide carbohydrates: fruits, honey, corn, rice, potatoes, bread, cereal, and noodles.

Your body needs *fats*. Fats give your body energy and provide certain vitamins. Fats also keep your skin smooth and healthy.

Here are some foods that provide fats: vegetable oils, butter, margarine, mayonnaise, ice cream, and avocados.

Your body needs *fiber.* Fiber helps your body digest its food. Fiber also helps keep your teeth clean and your gums healthy.

Here are some foods that provide fiber: raw fruits, vegetables, and whole grain cereals.

Your body needs *vitamins.* Vitamins help your body grow. Vitamins regulate how your body works. They also help your body resist certain sicknesses and diseases.

Here are some foods that are rich in vitamins: milk, eggs, wheat germ, yeast, fruits, vegetables, cereal, meat, fish, liver, and nuts.

Your body needs *minerals*. Minerals help your body form teeth and bones. They also help your body work properly.

Here are some foods that provide minerals: milk, cheese, eggs, meat, liver, dried fruits, fish, vegetables (especially the green leafy ones), and salt.

To make sure your body is getting enough of the
right foods, you need to eat the following every day:

- 2 fruits (one should be a citrus fruit)
- 2 vegetables (one should be dark green or deep
  yellow)
- 3 or more cups of milk (or servings of calcium-rich
  food)
- 2 or more servings of either cheese, eggs, beef,
  veal, pork, lamb, fish, poultry, dried beans, dried
  peas, or lentils
- 4 or more servings of whole grain, enriched or
  restored bread or cereal

Too much of some foods, such as sugar, salt, and fat, can hurt your body rather than help it. Thus, it is important to limit the amount of these foods you eat.

Your body needs *water.*

Your body consists mostly of water. Every day some of that water is lost through evaporation and bodily functions. You need to replenish the water in your body so that your body can continue to exist and function.

Water also helps keep your body's temperature even so your body does not get too hot or too cold.

To make sure your body is getting enough water, drink several glasses of water every day.

Your body needs *exercise.*

Exercise keeps your muscles in good condition so they can move your body. Exercise strengthens your tendons and ligaments so they remain flexible.

Exercise also helps your blood and other body fluids circulate food, water, and air to every part of your body.

You get some exercise by working and playing, but not enough. When you work and play, you use some of your muscles, but you do not use all of them.

This is why you need to do exercises. If you do the following exercises every day, you can be sure many of your muscles will get the use they need in order to be healthy and strong.

EXERCISE CHART

EXERCISE #	1	2	3	4	5	6	7	8	9	10	11	12
DAY 1	3	4	5	18	4	4	4	3	2	3	4	50
2	3	4	5	18	6	4	6	3	3	5	5	60
3	3	4	5	18	8	6	8	4	4	6	6	70
4	5	5	7	18	10	8	10	5	6	8	7	80
5	5	5	7	20	12	8	13	6	6	9	8	90
6	5	5	7	20	14	10	16	7	8	11	10	100
7	7	7	8	20	16	12	18	8	10	12	11	115
8	7	7	8	20	18	12	20	9	10	14	13	125
9	7	7	8	26	20	14	23	10	11	15	14	140
10	9	8	10	26	22	16	25	12	12	18	16	150
11	9	8	10	26	24	18	26	13	14	18	17	160
12	9	8	10	26	26	20	28	14	14	20	18	175
13	10	10	11	28	28	21	30	14	16	22	19	190
14	12	12	12	28	30	22	32	16	16	24	22	200

HMMM...

Exercise #1: Toe Touch

1. Stand tall with your feet together or slightly apart and your arms over your head.
2. Keeping your knees as straight as you can, bend forward and touch your toes.
3. Return to your starting position.
4. Each return to the starting position counts one.

Exercise #2: Knee Raise

1. Stand tall with your feet together and your arms down at your sides.
2. Keeping your back as straight as you can, grab your left knee and shin with your hands.
3. Pull your left leg up close to your body. Then put it back down on the floor.
4. Do the same thing with your right leg.
5. One left knee raise plus one right knee raise counts one.

Exercise #3: Side Bend

1. Stand tall with your feet about twelve inches apart. Bend your right arm over your head. Put your left hand on the side of your left thigh.
2. Keeping your back and knees as straight as you can, bend sideways. Move your left hand down your left leg as far as you can. Point left as far as you can with your right hand.
3. Return to your starting position, and change your arms (bend your left arm over your head and put your right hand on your right thigh).
4. One bend to the left plus one bend to the right counts one.

Exercise #4: Arm Circles

1. Stand tall with your feet about twelve inches apart and your arms at your sides.
2. Make backward circles with both arms at the same time. Then make forward circles with both arms at the same time.
3. Do half of your arm circles backward and half of them forward.
4. Each full arm circle counts one.

Exercise #5: Rocking Sit-Up

1. Lie down on the floor with your arms at your sides. Bend your knees and put your feet together on the floor, as close to your buttocks as you can get them.
2. Keeping your feet flat on the floor, slide them away from your hips as far as you can.
3. Without raising your feet, raise your upper body or torso until you are sitting.
4. Reach down and touch your toes with your fingers.
5. Return to your starting position.
6. Each return to the starting position counts one.

Exercise #6: Head and Leg Raise

1. Lie face down on the floor with your arms along your sides. Tuck your hands under your legs.
2. Keeping both legs as straight as you can, lift your head, shoulders, and left leg as high as you can off the floor.
3. Do the same thing using your right leg.
4. Each head-shoulder-leg raise counts one.

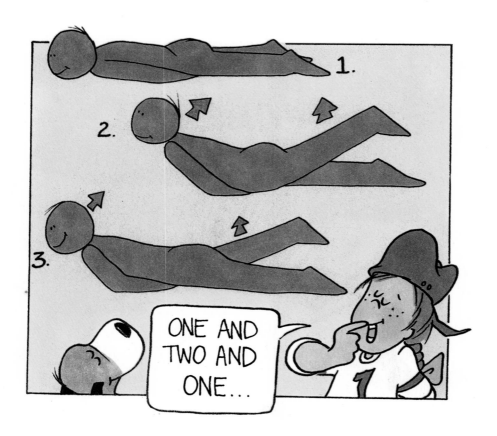

Exercise #7: Side Leg Raise

1. Lie on your right side on the floor with your back and legs straight. Stretch your right arm on the floor past your head. Use your left arm to balance you.
2. Raise your left leg as high as you can. Then put it down again.
3. Roll over onto your left side. Do the same thing with your right leg.
4. Each leg raise counts one.

Exercise #8: Knee Push-Up

1. Lie face down on the floor with your legs straight and feet together. Put your hands on the floor under your shoulders.
2. Keeping your back as straight as you can and your hands and knees on the floor, push your body off the floor until your arms are straight.
3. Return to your starting position.
4. Each return to the starting position counts one.

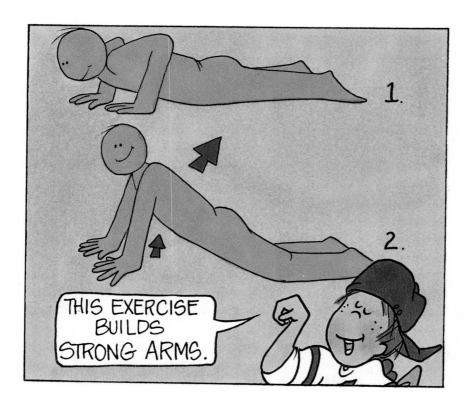

Exercise #9: Cross Over

1. Lie on your back with your legs straight and your feet together. Stretch your arms straight out at shoulder level.
2. Keep your right leg on the floor while you lift your left leg up and cross it over your body. Keep both shoulders touching the floor.
3. Touch the floor on the right side of your body with your left foot.
4. Return to your starting position. Then do the same thing with your right leg.
5. Each return to the starting position counts one.

Exercise #10: Posture Exercise

1. Lie on your back with your knees bent and your feet flat on the floor. Put your arms out to your side.
2. Press your back to the floor as hard as you can and then relax.
3. Each time your back presses to the floor counts one.

Exercise #11: Foot and Ankle Circles

1. Sit on the floor with your legs straight and your feet about fourteen inches apart. Put your hands on the floor behind you to help you sit up.
2. Point your toes away from your body as far as you can.
3. Point them toward your body as much as you can.
4. Relax your feet.
5. Each time your feet relax counts one.

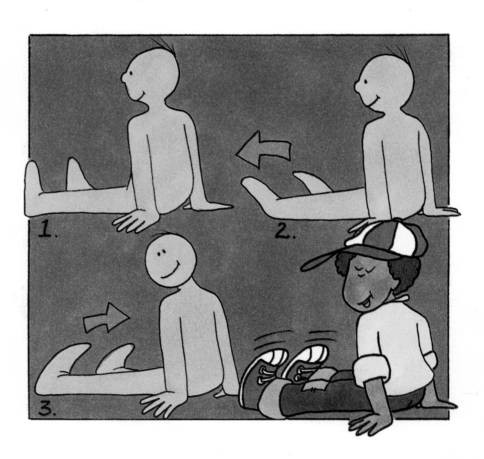

Exercise #12: Run and Jump in Place

1. Stand tall with your feet together and your hands at your sides.
2. Run in place.
3. Every time your left foot touches the floor counts one.
4. After fifty counts, jump up and down ten times.

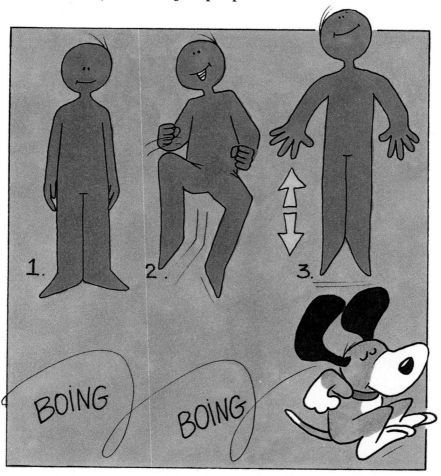

Your body needs *air and sunshine.*

Air provides the oxygen that your body needs to change food into energy.

Sunshine provides the vitamin D your body needs to make strong teeth and bones.

To make sure your body is getting enough air and
sunshine:

- Work and play outside in the fresh air and
  sunshine as often as possible.
- Do not put anything over your nose or mouth that
  will prevent you from breathing air (such as
  plastic bags).
- Do not get into anything that will have insufficient
  air for you to breathe (such as refrigerators,
  freezers, dryers, or closets).

Your body needs *proper clothing.* Clothes can protect your body from the weather.

You need to wear clothing that will protect your body from the sun because the sun can burn your skin. The sun can also dry up a lot of the needed moisture in your body.

You need to wear loose, lightweight clothing when the weather is hot. This kind of clothing allows air to circulate close to your body and cool it.

You need to wear warm clothes when the weather is cold. Your body must stay warm (approximately 98.6 degrees) so it will be comfortable and stay well.

You need to wear shoes to protect your feet. Your shoes should not be too large or too small. They need to fit your feet properly. Your feet are especially important because they must support the weight of your entire body.

Your body needs *adequate shelter.* Adequate shelter can protect you from hot weather.

Adequate shelter can protect you from cold weather.

Adequate shelter can protect you from natural disasters and other things that might threaten your life.

Take advantage of the shelter you have. Go inside and stay there if the weather or anything else might harm you in any way or cause you to get sick.

Your body needs to be *clean.* You need to keep your body clean because germs that cause disease and sickness grow in dirt.

Dirt can also clog openings in your skin. You need to wash your entire body every day to wash away the dirt that contains germs.

You need to wash your hair regularly because dirt from your hair can get into your scalp, eyes, and ears causing infections.

Wash your hands before you eat. Dirt from your hands can get on to your food. When you eat the food, the germs get inside your body. These germs can cause you to get sick.

Brush and floss your teeth after eating because food particles left on your teeth can cause your teeth to decay.

Decayed teeth cannot do the job they are supposed to do. Also, germs from decayed teeth can spread disease throughout your body.

Your body needs *rest and sleep.* Rest and sleep give your body a chance to get rid of body waste. They also give your body time to repair itself and grow.

Rest and sleep allow your body to build up energy. If you do not get enough sleep, you can become cranky. You might also become sick because disease germs attack a tired person more easily than a rested one.

To make sure that your body is getting enough rest
and sleep:

- Take time during the day to sit or lie down and
  rest your body.
- Sleep at least nine or ten hours every night.

Taking care of your body is one of the most important things you can do because it's the only one you have!